T0333368

STAR TREK™
KIRK FU
MANUAL

STAR TREK™
KIRK FU MANUAL

A GUIDE TO STARFLEET'S MOST FEARED MARTIAL ART

WRITTEN BY DAYTON WARD

ILLUSTRATIONS BY CHRISTIAN CORNIA

TITAN BOOKS

London

An Insight Editions Book

▶▶ *DEDICATED WITH SINCERE RESPECT
TO THE ONE AND ONLY*
WILLIAM SHATNER

CONTENTS

INTRODUCTION

As a senior cadet, you've already been subjected to training in a variety of martial arts subjects and disciplines that may seem at odds with Starfleet's mission of peaceful exploration. The expansion of knowledge to be shared by all the worlds of the Federation is indeed our mandate, as is our desire to venture ever farther into the universe while extending the hand of friendship, rather than the muzzle of a weapon. But that exploration has not always come easy, and neither has it come without cost.

The Federation has discovered numerous benevolent civilizations since Starfleet first undertook its mission to travel to the distant stars and explore those strange new worlds that awaited us. Along the way, we've also come across more than a few adversaries. Though we were able to forge eventual understanding, if not outright friendship with some of these races, others are committed to remaining our enemy. It is because of these unfortunate encounters that we must always be prepared not just to defend ourselves, but also to protect our interests within the ever-growing interstellar community.

Your instructors have familiarized you with a number of weapons, both Starfleet issue as well as those of a number of allied and adversarial races. Along the way, you've also been taught various methods of unarmed combat. Some might question the need for proficiency in such archaic means of self-defense. I suspect many of those critics have never faced off against a Klingon when one's phaser has been lost or rendered useless. They've likely never found themselves trapped on a distant world and forced to fight for their survival and for the entertainment of alien captors.

Until now, you've been undertaking Starfleet's standard unarmed combat training, which is an amalgam of methods gleaned from various martial arts practices from Earth and other Federation worlds. You've also been introduced to particular disciplines that you're liable to encounter during your Starfleet careers: *Suus Mahna,* an ancient defensive fighting style that originated on Vulcan, and the *Mok'bara*, a combat form that can be traced back thousands of years on the Klingon home world but is only now being given attention here at the Academy.

As for what you'll find in this training manual? The techniques contained in these pages are a distillation of skills I've acquired over the course of my own career. Some of them are born of methods I learned right here at the Academy, just as you have, while others are the products of improvisation in the face of necessity or even desperation. These methods have saved my life on more than one occasion. Should you ever find yourself in similarly dire straits, I hope you'll be ready to face such a challenge.

James T Kirk

PURPOSE

This publication is an addendum to Starfleet Manual SFM-9426, *Starfleet Unarmed Combat Training Program*, Revision 047, as distributed on stardate 6906.03. It is intended as a reference for all Starfleet personnel in the development of individual-unit, unarmed combat training programs. Its purpose is to guide Starfleet training officers and martial arts instructors in the proper techniques, procedures, tactics, and applications of unarmed combat skills.

The techniques as outlined in SFM-9426-K1 are meant to ensure the standard execution of these methods throughout Starfleet. This publication is not intended as a replacement for supervision by appropriate ship, station, or other unit commanders, or formal training by certified instructors.

⚠ WARNING

The methods presented in this manual can cause serious injury or death, particularly if employed in variable-gravity environments or against life-forms with physiologies that prove resistant to such measures.

Practical application in the teaching of these techniques will be conducted in strict accordance with established Starfleet training and safety procedures and only under the supervision of certified instructor personnel.

Admiral Heihachiro Nogura
DIRECTOR OF THE STARFLEET COMMAND

7410.12
STARDATE

BASIC DEFENSIVE STANCE

Most of these techniques begin with what is commonly referred to as the basic defensive stance. This position allows for a number of mid- or close-range defensive or offensive strikes and is also the foundation for more advanced training involving weapons.

Step 1: Place feet shoulder width apart. Take a half step forward with the left* foot. Turn hips and shoulders approximately forty-five degrees. Bend knees slightly and adjust footing in order to evenly distribute weight.

Step 2: Tuck elbows to the sides of the body. Raise hands to chin level to protect the head and face without hindering vision.

Step 3: Lower chin and stoop slightly, allowing arms and shoulders to provide protection for the neck and throat.

*The techniques described in this manual are written for right-handed application. To train left-handed, reverse references to "left" and "right" in the descriptions. To achieve complete proficiency, students should train to develop their techniques for both right- and left-handed execution.

STANDARD KARATE CHOP

Starfleet is an ever-evolving organization, its diversity represented by officers hailing from dozens of Federation worlds. But some aspects of Starfleet Academy training still tend to emphasize humanoid if not outright human sensibilities. Part of this is inescapable practicality, given the sheer number of species that seem to fall into this rather broad category. For all the wondrous differences to be found among the numerous races we regularly encounter, we're also brought together by the traits we share.

When it comes to unarmed combat, many of the techniques you learn in training are meant to be employed against humanoid opponents. Study of various species Starfleet has encountered over more than a century of deep-space exploration has shown that many of these races have physiologies with points of vulnerability similar to those of humans. Klingons, though stronger than the average human, are still susceptible to attack. The neck, for example, despite the typically thicker spinal column, presents a "soft spot" alongside the larynx that can be exploited.

On the other hand, such a weakness may be mitigated if your humanoid aggressor is possessed by forces beyond their conscious control, such as an alien energy being, or if they're somehow imbued with godlike powers and strength. This was the case with my dear friend Gary Mitchell who, after exposure to a bizarre energy field at the edge of our galaxy, began mutating both physically and mentally.

In addition to developing heightened psionic and telekinetic abilities, Mitchell's strength also increased far beyond that of even the most robust human. I learned that the hard way when I ended up facing off against him. It took every bit of my training—along with no small amount of improvisation and desperation—to survive that confrontation. That included strikes such as this one, though Mitchell shrugged off most of my attempts as though I had never touched him.

As is the case with most offensive and defensive strikes, you need speed along with accuracy and force during this part of the engagement in order to gain advantage over your opponent and bring an end to the encounter as quickly as possible.

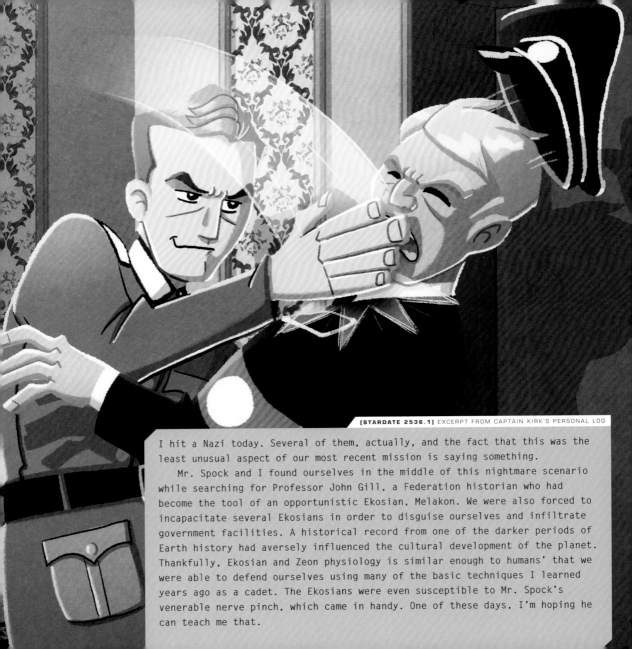

I hit a Nazi today. Several of them, actually, and the fact that this was the least unusual aspect of our most recent mission is saying something.

Mr. Spock and I found ourselves in the middle of this nightmare scenario while searching for Professor John Gill, a Federation historian who had become the tool of an opportunistic Ekosian, Melakon. We were also forced to incapacitate several Ekosians in order to disguise ourselves and infiltrate government facilities. A historical record from one of the darker periods of Earth history had aversely influenced the cultural development of the planet. Thankfully, Ekosian and Zeon physiology is similar enough to humans' that we were able to defend ourselves using many of the basic techniques I learned years ago as a cadet. The Ekosians were even susceptible to Mr. Spock's venerable nerve pinch, which came in handy. One of these days, I'm hoping he can teach me that.

STANDARD KARATE CHOP

▶▶ This technique will vary in effectiveness depending on your opponent's physiology and whether they are an unwilling host to a parasitic alien entity or have metamorphosed into a godlike being. Unpredictable results should be expected.

Step 1: From the basic defensive stance, close with opponent. Lead with whichever leg is opposite the striking hand, and plant that foot as you step into the attack.

Step 2: Raise leading, nonstriking arm to defend again a possible counterattack. Draw back striking hand, extending an joining fingers and tuckin thumb alongside the forefinger. Raise striking hand while rotating shoulder and hip away from opponent.

Step 3: Thrust striking hand into opponent's neck while rotating shoulder and hip forward. Rotate wrist so that palm is up, and strike target with your hand's outer edge.

Step 4: Follow through the target location with striking hand before returning to the basic defensive stance.

SECTION 02

SLIPPERY EEL

A fundamental aspect of unarmed combat is the ability to break free of an opponent's hold on you, regardless of differences in size or strength. The ability to extricate yourself from such situations is vital if you hope to control any confrontation. Here, you can truly exploit your training and skills.

The most significant aspect of breaking an opponent's hold is the speed by which you can get free. The longer an adversary has you under their control, the more time there is for you to be subdued, incapacitated, severely injured, or even killed. Your opponent may have reinforcements, turning the engagement into a numbers game you can't win.

Such was the case when I found myself fighting alternate versions of my crewmembers from a similar but markedly different parallel universe. Though I was outnumbered, they were unfamiliar with the unorthodox method I used to break free from a security guard's grip. I then applied more conventional techniques in order to gain the advantage.

Of course, breaking holds is just one part of a successful self-defense. Should you find yourself in the clutches of an enemy, it's critical that you free yourself with all possible speed so that you can press your attack or resistance.

Several martial arts disciplines teach different methods for escaping holds. As with the other unarmed combat techniques you've learned from your instructors, escaping a hold in a real fight will always involve factors that never present themselves in a training scenario. You'll learn to identify and even anticipate these variables as your skills improve, and you'll adapt your fighting style accordingly.

[STARDATE 3726.4] EXCERPT FROM CAPTAIN KIRK'S PERSONAL LOG

It's strange fighting a member of your own crew. They don't tell you about that at the Academy. During my tenure as captain of the *Enterprise*, I've had the unfortunate occasion to fight members of my own crew, even including my first officer, Mr. Spock. One thing about combat with fellow Starfleet officers is that—generally speaking—they have at least some of the same training you possess. Every member of Starfleet is required to remain proficient in these skills, but as with anything else, talent and level of expertise varies. This is one of the reasons I always advocate for continual training and practice in these skills. If I'm going to face off against an opponent like Spock, or someone else whose strength or skill rivals or exceeds mine, I want to be ready.

SLIPPERY EEL

▶▶ Starfleet Academy unarmed combat instructors were unable to re-create this technique in a training environment. In all honesty, we're stumped.

Step 2: Vigorously wiggle your arm in a ninety-degree arc back and forth, left to right. Once attacker's grip loosens, jerk your arm free.

Step 1: As opponent seizes your arm, plant feet shoulder width apart. Keep knees bent in order to evenly distribute weight, and extend the arm held by your adversary. Keep arm parallel to the ground.

Step 3: Once arm is free, rotate hips so that your back is to opponent. With freed arm, tuck and drive your elbow into attacker's midsection.

Step 4: Push back and away from opponent. Assume the basic defensive stance. From here, you can defend against another attack or initiate a counterattack.

DOUBLE CLUTCH

M ost unarmed combat methods are built on striking your opponent with one hand while leading or defending with your other hand. Underpinning that practice is the idea that the primary goal of self-defense is to prevent against being struck. You train to control the distance you maintain from your adversary, remaining out of their reach until you're ready to strike.

Unfortunately, reality only rarely unfolds in accordance with training scenarios.

The simple truth is that real-life skirmishes often stray from the clean, practiced techniques your instructors have labored to instill in their students. Irregularities are particularly common the longer a fight continues, as well as in cases when your opponent has training very different from yours or no formal combat training at all. There also is the unfortunate possibility that your adversary's strength or technical skills are much greater than yours. These are among the several reasons that your training emphasizes quick, decisive conclusion to unarmed engagements.

Still, things often don't work out as you think or hope they will. Such was the case when I found myself battling a genetically augmented human, Khan Noonien Singh. A product of twentieth-century eugenics, Khan possessed strength equivalent to five normal humans. His weakness was in underestimating his opponents based solely on the mental and physical inferiority that he perceived.

That said, he came dangerously close to killing me in my own ship's engineering room. How did I avoid that? To put it bluntly, I played dirty. Despite my lesser strength, I was able to utilize my own fighting skills and even understanding of my surroundings—my engineering skills, in this case, paired with the equipment and tools that were within easy reach—while exploiting Khan's misjudgment of my ability to defeat him. Even then, I had to put all my strength into one solid, double-handed punch to his kidneys just to get him to slow down.

Sometimes, you're forced to rely on whatever brute-force methods you can muster to get the job done.

m sore. All over. I guess that's
 be expected when you fight a
netically enhanced human.

 There can be no denying Khan's
perior intellect, or that of
s followers, who represent
at was once believed to be the
st humanity had to offer. With
eir enhanced physiologies and
tellect, they were intended
 usher in a new era of human
olution—one perhaps better
ited to the rigors of exploring,
lonizing, and surviving distant
rlds throughout the galaxy. Of
urse, as Mr. Spock put it, their
eators failed to acknowledge
e time-tested proverb, "Superior
ility breeds superior ambition."
 And yes, they can sure throw a
nch.

 It took every bit of training,
ill, and strength I had to stand
e to toe with Khan, and even
en I had to resort to tricks
d a bit of luck to beat him. By
e time I finally put him down
ng enough to have him taken into
stody, I could barely walk.
ery muscle in my body hurts, and
obably will for the next week.

 Here's hoping I never run into
an again.

DOUBLE CLUTCH

▶▶ This technique is intended as a strike against your adversary's vulnerable organs located in the lower torso. Of course, this is based on training against humanoid opponents. Results may vary against nonhumanoid rivals or humanoids with more robust physiologies (Klingons, Romulans, etc.). Employ at your discretion.

Step 1: From the basic defensive stance, close with opponent. Step forward into the attack, planting right foot.

Step 2: Clasping hands together and interlocking fingers, rotate shoulders and hips away from your leading leg. Pull arms back while maintaining the two-handed grip.

Step 3: Rotating hips and shoulders toward opponent, swing arms forward, targeting the area between opponent's hips and the lower edge of their rib cage.

Step 4: Follow through the target location with striking hand before stepping back and returning to the basic defensive stance.

HEAD BUTT

As you've trained to protect yourself and dispatch your opponent in hand-to-hand combat, your instructors have taught you that the often chaotic nature of these encounters requires adapting and improvising. Perhaps you're injured, or your opponent is just stronger or better trained than you are. Or perhaps—like when I was forced to fight in an arena on Triskelion—your hands are tied behind your back, making hand-to-hand combat a bit more of a challenge.

Proper instruction and the reflexes you hone during training can help you in these situations, but the simple truth, at least as I see it based on hard-won experience, is that you have to seize whatever opportunity presents itself in order to prevail. Sometimes, that means grabbing whatever object is available and using it as a weapon. On other occasions, it might entail unconventional methods, including those that go against everything you've been trained to do.

And then, there are those times when you literally just use your head.

Let me be the first to warn you that employing a head butt is not the most tactically sound means of striking your opponent. Most importantly, it presents a risk to you if your adversary's bone structure is denser than that of a typical humanoid; a warrior-caste Klingon comes to mind. But if you're able to stun your opponent, even for a few seconds, you can usually gain an opening and bring your training to bear. I tend to think of it as an action of last resort, so I caution you: If you're going to use your head in these situations, be smart about it.

[STARDATE 3212.9] EXCERPT FROM CAPTAIN KIRK'S PERSONAL LOG

A vacation wouldn't exactly go unappreciated right about now.

Upon our kidnapping into the brutal gladiator school on the planet Triskelion, I quickly realized our fellow slaves, or "drill thralls," and their fighting abilities were not to be underestimated. While I think our Starfleet training gave us some advantage in surviving the early days of our captivity, I have no doubt that over time, our injuries, the superior opponent, and even random chance eventually would have seen to our deaths.

On the other hand, I also realized that we could overcome the thralls, and even their Providers, through noncombative means. The thralls had never known life beyond slavery. Because they had nothing to truly fight for—aside from their masters—they had nothing else for which they felt compelled to live . . . or die.

We did.

Step 1: This strike assumes you are already closely engaged with your opponent: within reach with arms interlocked.

Step 2: Plant your feet shoulder width apart. Bend knees and lean forward, distributing body weight until your head is below opponent's chin.

Ow.

Step 3: Snap head up and back, with sufficient strength to strike opponent's chin. Follow through the strike as adversary's head is forced backward.

Step 4: Use arms to push back and away from opponent, and return to basic defensive stance. Before adversary can recover, be prepared to launch a more effective, targeted strike to end the engagement.

BOX LUNCH

I f you're assigned to a starship that's tasked with exploring uncharted worlds, and you encounter a new species, peaceful contact is naturally the primary goal. But on occasion, you're sure to find yourselves at odds with a previously unknown race. In these situations, your training may not always be useful, given the emphasis on defending against humanoid adversaries. Sometimes, you don't discover the limits of your training until you're already facing off against an unfamiliar opponent.

And that's before we get into the idea of you being manipulated by an advanced alien race and forced to fight for your very life. This often ends up being a form of entertainment for such beings, but every so often, it can be for their education, as well. You may not always be able to discern the difference— at least not while you're just trying to stay alive. On these occasions, other aspects of your Starfleet training will prove invaluable, along with the values and ethos you embody by wearing your uniform and acting as representatives of the Federation.

Such was the case when I found myself forced to fight an intelligent, bipedal reptilian known as a Gorn. Though our intellects were likely on an equal footing, the Gorn more than outmatched me when it came to physical strength. I had the edge in speed and agility, but that didn't prevent me from ending up in close combat with this newly encountered alien.

It's important to remember that, while parts of your self-defense training won't be effective against every alien race, certain physiological elements tend to be universal. Most living beings possess visual or auditory organs that are vulnerable to attack. While strikes to these targets may not be lethal or even incapacitating, they may give you precious seconds to mount a stronger defense. Remember: Adaptability, quick thinking, and improvisation are key to survival.

[STARDATE 3047.1] EXCERPT FROM CAPTAIN KIRK'S PERSONAL

We're a most promising species, I'm told. I've always believed this, of course, but it's nice to receive independent confirmation once in a while.

In the heat of conflict against the Gorn captain, I had some old lessons reinforced. I should probably send a note of thanks to my Academy instructors for the hours spent drilling those hand-to hand techniques into my thick skull. They've saved my life a few times, and this was one of them.

Of greater importance, however, are the larger lessons about rushing to the worst of conclusions about someone you hardly know. It's humbling to realize you've allowed your instinctive biases to cloud your judgment, particularly when that prejudice almost results in loss of life. I can only hope the Gorn captain I fought has had cause for similar reflection. Otherwise, the colonists on Cestus III, killed by the Gorn following a tragic misunderstanding, will truly have died in vain.

Step 1: From the basic defensive stance, close with opponent. Step forward into the attack, planting the right foot. Keep feet shoulder width apart (unless you are shorter than your opponent and you are lifted off the ground).

Step 2: Raise arms so that hands are level with adversary's head. (This is also the starting position if you are already closely engaged with opponent, inside their reach with arms interlocked, and attempting to break free.) Draw back hands, extending and joining fingers and tucking thumbs alongside forefingers. Slightly cup each hand.

If you've reached this point and discovered that your opponent (a) has no ears or similar openings, or (b) is not affected by this technique, then we don't know what to tell you. Maybe you should've just gone for the karate chop.

Step 3: Thrust cupped hands against opponent's ears or other auditory organs. If no such organs are visible, aim for the area approximating the temples on a human or humanoid.

Step 4: As opponent reacts to the strike, push away and return to the basic defensive stance.

TIBERIUS TWIST

ere's something they don't typically teach you during your Academy self-defense courses: Noncorporeal beings are tough to fight.

I'm not even talking about using phasers against them, though that sort of thing presents its own unique challenges. What if the entity in question doesn't register on sensors? How do you target something your weapons can't detect or target? What if the being's not visible at all, to either technology or the naked eye? What do you do then?

And even if you can find or see them, that doesn't mean you can fight them. Perhaps they're immune to energy weapons or possess their own version of cloaking technology. What if they're able to shift themselves out of our space-time continuum at will, dodging—in a very real, interdimensional sense—whatever you throw at them?

Yes, it happened. More than once.

Of course, there are some varieties of noncorporeal life that can assume material form by taking control over the body of a sentient, living being. I've encountered a few of those during my time in Starfleet.

Aggressors in these situations may possess superior strength. On the other hand, their unfamiliarity with the limitations of physical bodies may make them vulnerable. Regardless, it's not about who is the stronger individual.

Using opponents' mass and movements against them is a fundamental aspect of many unarmed combat and martial arts techniques. By themselves, methods such as the Tiberius Twist (also known as the reverse wrist throw) aren't necessarily intended to incapacitate an adversary. Instead, they're a means of thwarting an attack while avoiding injury. They also provide an opportunity for you to put some space between you and your rival so that you can either seek retreat or prepare for a more direct defense.

...body who joins Starfleet has to expect to run into
...ngs that are unusual, unexplained, and perhaps
...elievable. But, Jack the Ripper? Who saw that coming?
...Our visit to Argelius II was supposed to be an
...eventful shore leave on a planet where violence is all
...anathema to the indigenous population. The planet's
...putation as one of the most benevolent and welcoming
...stinations in the galaxy is well earned, and it's
...rtbreaking that such peace was shattered by something
...n of pure evil. That's the only way I know to describe
...e noncorporeal entity Redjac.
...The only reason we were able to identify and capture
...was because it took over the body of Mr. Hengist, the
...ef city administrator on Argelius II. I fought Redjac
...le he controlled the man's body, and it was a skirmish
...ikely would've lost if not for my training.

TIBERIUS TWIST

▸▸ This technique is even more effective in low- or variable-gravity environments.

Step 1: From the basic defensive stance, close with opponent. Step forward into the attack, planting the right foot. Use left leg to establish leverage against adversary.

Step 2: Reach with both hands for opponent's leading arm. With your leading, nonstriking hand, grip adversary's forearm just below the elbow. Use dominant, striking hand to grip opponent's wrist.

Step 3: With feet braced, rotate opponent's arm away from you. To avoid injury, adversary will move in that direction, providing you with sufficient momentum to carry through the twist and flip opponent off their feet. Follow through with the movement until adversary is on the ground, lying face up.

Step 4: Move away from opponent and return to the basic defensive stance.

SECTION 07

HIP THROW

As with the reverse wrist throw, or Tiberius Twist, the hip throw allows you to use your opponent's mass against them. Such moves give you options for quickly seizing the initiative during a confrontation, either to escape, withdraw and regroup, or just gain space and time to ready for a defensive or even offensive strike.

My Starfleet training didn't help me much in my fight with a Mugato on Zeta Boötis III, though it did later benefit me when I was dealing with some of the local villagers who'd fallen in league with a Klingon agent. Hip throws in particular came in handy, along with a few other tricks I've picked up over the years.

The hip throw is a comparatively simple move to master, as it is effective against most humanoid life-forms regardless of size or strength. It is especially effective against adversaries who possess no formal unarmed combat training and as such may not know how to judge an opponent's body language while delivering their own attack or defense.

Techniques like this rely less on your own physical strength and more on your ability to anticipate and react to your opponent's movements. Your instructors have already introduced you to these sorts of defensive measures, as well as to the importance of practice: This training teaches you how to avoid injuring yourself, but repetition will give you confidence should you ever find yourself in an actual confrontation.

[STARDATE 4212.3] EXCERPT FROM CAPTAIN KIRK'S PERSONAL LOG

Here's something else they should probably incorporate into Starfleet unarmed combat training: You have to adapt your methods when your opponent possesses no formal skills of their own. Indeed, unarmed combat against an untrained opponent carries its own set of risks. An inexperienced adversary should never be underestimated, precisely because their lack of instruction brings with it an element of unpredictability that can be dangerous during a confrontation. In my case, it applied to representatives of a preindustrial civilization as well as not one but two members of indigenous lower-order mammals.

Step 1: From the basic defensive stance, as opponent approaches, take one half step forward and plant right foot. Keep knees bent in order to evenly distribute your weight. Rotate hips forty-five degrees away from adversary.

Step 2: Upon contact with oncoming opponent, tuck right hand under adversary's armpit. Use left hand to brace and guide attacker's torso as the throw begins.

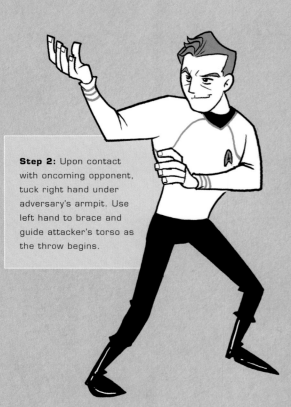

If your adversary has more than two arms, tuck your hand under their lowest extremity.

Results may vary if your opponent is a shapeshifter.

Step 3: Using opponent's momentum, pull them along with you as you continue rotating your hips away from them. Once attacker's feet leave the ground, follow through with the throw, pulling opponent across your hip and directing them toward the ground.

Step 4: As adversary lands on the ground, return to the basic defensive stance.

LATERAL BODY BLOCK

Despite your training, it's not realistic to believe that you can fare well against multiple opponents in a lengthy confrontation. In most circumstances, you can face perhaps two, sometimes three adversaries before their numbers overcome your skills. During such engagements, your goal should be to disable, disengage, and seek retreat as quickly as possible.

I once found myself fighting three United States Air Force officers while I was infiltrating a top-secret military installation, after the *Enterprise* was thrown back in time to twentieth-century Earth. We were there trying to remove any evidence of our presence in that time period, when we were discovered. My main priority during this particular fight was to buy time for Mr. Sulu to escape to the ship and avoid seriously injuring any of the servicemen, for fear of somehow altering the timeline. I gave up most of my formal combat training in favor of simple diversion tactics, designed to engage all three of them for as long as possible. My strategy worked, at least so far as helping Mr. Sulu get away. I was taken into custody, but Mr. Spock was there to bail me out of trouble. Again.

When fighting multiple attackers, the key to success is to use at least one of your opponents against the others. This usually requires you to close with and latch onto your chosen opponent, then place that opponent between you and the others. From this position, you can disable one of the other adversaries. But even then, you run the risk of extending the encounter and allowing their superior numbers to overwhelm you.

I've learned that the faster you can put most if not all of your attackers off their feet, the greater your chance of extricating yourself or at least defending yourself one-on-one with each opponent. For this to work, you must take control of the situation rather than wait to react.

[STARDATE 3114.7] EXCERPT FROM CAPTAIN KIRK'S PERSONAL LOG

Sometimes, even I don't honestly know what I'm going to do during a fight.

It's true. Sometimes I'm just doing whatever I can, either to end the confrontation quickly or create an opening to retreat long enough to come up with a better plan.

Our close-combat instructors tried to warn us about this sort of thing at least once during my training. Maybe they never came out and said it in plain language, but they certainly hinted at it. I guess it's why they used to emphasize the importance of adaptability to your surroundings.

Step 1: From the basic defensive stance, close the distance to opponents until you are two paces away. Plant leading foot.

Step 2: Follow through the stride and push off with leading foot. Extend arms and angle body forty-five degrees to adversaries as you approach.

While attempting to re-create this technique, Starfleet Academy instructors concluded that it works best if your opponents decide to begin falling backward on their own just before you make bodily contact. Your results may vary.

Step 3: Strike chosen opponent with your torso, using momentum to push through the attack and cast adversary backward, off-balance, and into their companions.

Step 4: Recover from the attack, retreat from adversaries, and resume the basic defensive stance.

ROLLING THUNDER

You've likely noticed by now that the techniques we've covered have one thing in common: They're primarily intended for fighting unarmed adversaries. The methods you've learned so far can be employed against strikes from blade or blunt-force weapons, but the injury risk does increase in dramatic fashion.

If you're forced to act against an armed aggressor, seizing the initiative is still the key to success. You must also remember that in some situations, your opponent may brandish a weapon to compensate for lack of formal unarmed combat training.

This was certainly true of the inhabitants of Gamma Trianguli VI. In an extraordinary example of an arrested, preindustrial culture, the natives there lived and toiled in service to a millennia-old machine, Vaal, which they viewed as their god. The people knew nothing except what the machine communicated to them, and upon seeing me and my landing party as a threat, Vaal set his people against us. Though they had no real fighting skills, the machine showed them how to employ heavy clubs against us.

In this case, having a move that can be employed against an attacker wielding a weapon proved to be a valuable asset. With the native population holding their clubs high above their heads, the only alternative was to go low. Moves like this were what helped give us the edge in the fight.

So, while you likely possess at least some advantage in situations such as this, it's critical that you not underestimate your enemy. Their determination, along with random chance or simple bad luck, can still end up being a danger to you.

[STARDATE 3717.4] EXCERPT FROM CAPTAIN KIRK'S PERSONAL LOG

I honestly do take the Prime Directive seriously. Have I violated that rule? On occasion. Have I done so lightly, or without considering the ramifications of my actions? Of course not.

Freeing a subjugated people from a machine that's arrested their societal development for thousands of years after that machine's builders have died blurs the lines in a way I'm mostly comfortable with. In order to show them a better way of life, we unfortunately introduced them to some harsh concepts. There's the simple difference between life and death, of course, but there is also fighting for survival and killing indiscriminately at someone else's command. I hope our efforts on Gamma Trianguli VI end up helping those people, rather than hurting them. I guess we'll have to wait and see.

Step 1: From the basic defensive stance, as opponent approaches, close the distance until you are five paces away. Plant leading foot.

Step 2: Pushing off with the feet, lower shoulder and follow it into a modified forward roll toward adversary, aiming for their legs.

This technique requires precision timing and accuracy. You may not get a chance to pick up the spare, so act accordingly.

Step 3: Upon making contact with opponent, continue the roll through them as your shoulder strikes the ground, knocking attacker's feet out from under them and causing them to fall forward.

Step 4: As you roll through the attack and past the adversary, regain your feet, face adversary, and resume the basic defensive stance.

FLYING DROP KIRK

Most of the fighting methods to which you've been exposed involve striking or defending with your hands and arms. But it's important to remember that at the beginning of any fight, legs are another option for quickly defeating your opponent. Kicks, when executed with proper speed and power, can easily disrupt an adversary's attack. With sufficient force, you can injure or incapacitate in short order. You must move faster than your opponent, before they're able to ready their own defense.

This includes adversaries you're not even certain are real.

If you've studied some of our *Enterprise* missions, you know about our encounter with the Melkotians. After we unwittingly offended them by venturing into their space, one of their representatives subjected us to an illusory experience in which we re-created the events leading up to the deadly gunfight at the O.K. Corral in Tombstone, Arizona, on nineteenth-century Earth. Everything we were experiencing was little more than an elaborate simulation created by the Melkotians. But so long as we believed we could be injured or killed, that was a real possibility.

Once Spock used his telepathic abilities to assist us in overcoming this fear, we were able to confront our adversaries using more conventional methods. I'm happy to report that I was able to defeat my imaginary opponent using a kick like the one described here. It put me on the immediate offensive, giving "Wyatt Earp" no chance to establish a formidable defense, let alone launch any attack of his own. Remember, to succeed with tactics such as these, initiative, speed, and audacity are your allies.

[STARDATE 4386.5] EXCERPT FROM CAPTAIN KIRK'S PERSONAL LOG

Who knew you could hurt so much from fighting an optical illusion?

Is that really what happened during our encounter with the Melkotians? Even now that we're on our way to begin negotiations with them following the "test" they put us through, I still don't know for certain what happened. Mr. Spock assures me what we experienced was an illusion conjured by the Melkotians and presented to us in a manner not unlike telepathy. But, my body tells me that my landing party and I weren't simply standing there while this "joint hallucination" unfolded. My knuckles are sore in the same way they are after a real fight. That kick I gave Wyatt Earp sure felt real enough.

I kicked Wyatt Earp. Dropkicked him, even. How many of the encounters that we've had over the course of this mission already border on the unbelievable? This is just one more on an already impressive stack.

FLYING DROP KIRK

▶▶ Technique requires exact timing, accuracy, and balance. Results will vary in low- or null-gravity environments.

Step 1: Run toward opponent, closing the distance until you are three paces away. Plant leading foot.

Step 2: Pushing off with feet, jump up, and angle feet toward adversary, putting weight behind your legs.

Step 3: As you strike opponent, continue through attack as they are pushed backward and off their own feet.

Step 4: You will likely fall to the ground at the end of this strike. Regain your footing, face adversary, and resume the basic defensive stance.

JIMMY WALL BANGER

The methods discussed until this point are all designed for when you have no weapons of your own, though their application is largely the same regardless of whether your opponent is armed. Your next phase of training will incorporate combat techniques utilizing close-quarters weapons such as knives, staffs, and clubs.

However, it's important to remember that in an actual confrontation, you may not have the luxury of using weapons with which you've received extensive instruction. Experienced close-combat teachers will be the first to tell you that improvisation can be the difference between victory and defeat. What does this mean? For one thing, it might entail using whatever object you find in the immediate vicinity during a fight: a rock or piece of wood or some item sitting on a table or shelf.

But a wall?

I'll be the first to admit that this is perhaps the most unconventional technique you'll learn during this phase of your training. It wasn't the result of a conscious decision on my part; it was just something born from the desperation of the moment, and it happened to work out in my favor.

The Andorian—rather, what I thought at the time was an Andorian—took me almost completely by surprise. Only instinct and training saved me from falling immediate victim to his attack. Everything else after that is something of a blur.

From the beginning of the attack, I knew that something was off about my assailant. He didn't possess the skill I'd come to expect from Andorians with military training. Only after the Andorian was revealed to be an Orion spy in disguise did it all finally make sense. An unusual opponent sometimes calls for an equally unusual move.

[STARDATE 3844.5] EXCERPT FROM CAPTAIN KIRK'S PERSONAL LOG

A knife through the ribs is something to be avoided. To be fair, it's not exactly the sort of thing I ever expected to worry about all that much. I'd read enough about earlier exploration missions to know this wasn't completely out of the question, but it's still a surprise when it happens to you. It's even more disturbing when you're the captain and it happens aboard your own ship.

So, now I'm lying here in sickbay. Dr. McCoy is insufferably pleased with himself that he has both Spock and me here, under bed rest orders for the next two days.

JIMMY WALL BANGER

▸▸ This technique requires precise timing, accuracy, and direction of energy. Results will vary in low- or null-gravity environments.

Step 2: Bring feet together to strike the wall with your heels. Bend knees to absorb the force of the impact.

Step 1: From the basic defensive stance—and assuming opponent is near a wall or other solid, vertical surface—run toward the adversary. Close the distance until you are two paces away before planting leading foot and pushing off, angling for the section of wall or other vertical surface adjacent to opponent's position.

Step 3: Push off from the wall with your feet, angling body toward opponent. Strike adversary with shoulders and upper back.

Step 4: Along with the adversary, you will almost certainly fall to the ground at the conclusion of this strike. Before opponent can recover, regain feet, face adversary, and resume the basic defensive stance.

THE JTKO

One of the key tenets of unarmed combat is to always remain in control of your emotions. Just as courage is measured by an ability to manage fear during times of extreme stress, success in battle is also determined by the capacity to either control anger or channel such strong emotion into the energy needed to win.

Close-combat instructors caution that a lack of discipline over one's temper makes it all too easy to lose focus over skills and training. Instincts and judgment clouded by rage can be dangerous or even fatal. This is why instructors train beginning students almost to the point of exhaustion—to render them so fatigued that anger has nothing left to subvert. As students learn to control and even harness their feelings during training, they can do so reflexively during actual stressful situations. Then, the lessons absorbed in training, unfettered by pure passion, become almost second nature. Attacks and defensive tactics then spring from learned skill and expert application rather than brute force driven by blind rage or other unhelpful emotions.

Looking back at some of my past mission reports, I recall how many times I allowed or almost allowed my feelings to overwhelm me. I'm not proud of those moments, but I suppose they each served as learning opportunities, in their own ways. Lessons such as those are just as important as the physical aspects of unarmed combat training.

On the other hand, I'd be lying if I said there aren't times when a good solid roundhouse punch is just the best way to end a fight.

As the *Enterprise* departs the Omicron Delta region for our next assignment, our encounter with the mysterious "shore leave planet" has given me much to think about. The idea of an entire world with the sole purpose of catering to your every desire is interesting, but there's that old adage: Be careful what you wish for. Once we determined the truth behind the planet and it's power to bring any fantasy to life, the rest of the crew's shore leave proceeded without incident. However, my official report to Starfleet Command will include a recommendation that all vessels give this world a wide berth until it can be studied and better understood.

As for myself, reuniting with Ruth—even a facsimile of her—brought back a host of pleasant memories. And facing off against my old nemesis, Finnegan, was satisfying for completely different reasons. I know the whole thing is rather silly, and I'm even a little embarrassed that I allowed a fight with the artificial representation of an old enemy to drag on for as long as it did.

But it still felt pretty damned good.

THE JTKO

▶▶ This technique has varying results depending on your opponent's physiology, or if they're an artificial representation or even an illusion generated by aliens. Unpredictable results should be expected.

Step 2: Raise leading, nonstriking arm in order to defend against possible counterattack. Draw back striking hand and make fist, resting thumb along the first knuckles of index and middle fingers. Rotate shoulder and hip away from opponent.

Step 1: From the basic defensive stance, close with opponent. Plant the foot as you step into the attack.

Step 3: Thrust striking hand toward opponent's jaw while rotating shoulder and hip forward. Rotate wrist so that the heel of your hand faces downward, and strike.

Step 4: Follow through the target location with your fist as opponent falls backward, and return to the basic defensive stance.

SFM-9426-K1 ASSESSMENT QUESTIONS

Evaluate your knowledge of the techniques illustrated in SFM-9426-K1
by completing the following informal review:

1. The strike best suited to inflicting temporary discomfort to an opponent's auditory organs is the:
   A) Double Clutch
   B) Box Lunch
   C) Tiberius Twist
   D) Head butt

2. The best way to get under and past an armed opponent while avoiding injury to yourself is the:
   A) Slippery Eel
   B) Flying Drop Kirk
   C) Rolling Thunder
   D) Jimmy Wall Banger

3. When defending against multiple adversaries, your best option is the:
   A) Lateral body block
   B) Standard karate chop
   C) JTKO
   D) Hip throw

4. The strike best suited for attacking an opponent's torso and the vital organs (hopefully) found there is the:
   A) Rolling Thunder
   B) Double Clutch
   C) Tiberius Twist
   D) Box Lunch

5. This defensive strike can be effective if you're already engaged with your adversary, inside their reach with arms intertwined and looking to break free. It also hurts . . . you. This move is the:
   A) JTKO
   B) Jimmy Wall Banger
   C) Hip throw
   D) Head butt

6. What's one method of freeing an opponent's grip on your arm?
   A) Standard karate chop
   B) Tiberius Twist
   C) Slippery Eel
   D) Box Lunch

7. The best way to get an extra leg up against your adversary is with the:
   A) Double Clutch
   B) Flying Drop Kirk
   C) Rolling Thunder
   D) Lateral body block

8. One technique for using an aggressor's momentum against them is the:
   A) JTKO
   B) Slippery Eel
   C) Head butt
   D) Hip throw

9. For a master of unarmed combat, even your surroundings can be employed as a weapon. One defensive strike designed with this in mind is the:
   A) Box Lunch
   B) Jimmy Wall Banger
   C) Lateral body block
   D) Flying Drop Kirk

10. This common attack is designed to target a "soft spot" found in most humanoid physiologies:
    A) Slippery Eel
    B) Hip throw
    C) Standard karate chop
    D) Rolling Thunder

11. Take your enemy by the hand and show them a good time with this technique:
    A) Tiberius Twist
    B) Double Clutch
    C) Box Lunch
    D) Slippery Eel

12. It's the only way to bring a proper end to any confrontation:
    A) Lateral body block
    B) Jimmy Wall Banger
    C) Flying Drop Kirk
    D) JTKO

1. **B)** Box Lunch
2. **C)** Rolling Thunder
3. **A)** Lateral body block
4. **B)** Double Clutch
5. **D)** Head butt
6. **C)** Slippery Eel
7. **B)** Flying Drop Kirk
8. **D)** Hip throw
9. **B)** Jimmy Wall Banger
10. **C)** Standard karate chop
11. **A)** Tiberius Twist
12. **D)** JTKO

CONGRATULATIONS!

You have successfully completed your assessment and demonstrated exceptional proficiency in the skill of unarmed personal defense. As a Starfleet Academy cadet and potential future Starfleet officer, it falls to you to continue your training and improve your abilities. Further, you will soon be charged with imparting knowledge to the next generation of Starfleet officers. Employ this knowledge wisely and only in the appropriate situations, and inspire your subordinates to follow your sterling example.

UNITED FEDERATION OF PLANETS

* *

STARFLEET ACADEMY

CERTIFICATE OF TRAINING

This is to certify that

_____

in accordance with Starfleet regulations pertaining to the
instruction of academy cadets, has successfully completed the training
curriculum as put forth in Starfleet Field Manual.

SFM-9426-K1

STARFLEET UNARMED COMBAT TRAINING PROGRAM

KIRK ADDENDUM 1

Given at Starfleet Academy, San Francisco, California, Earth

STARDATE: _____

April

APRIL HEBERT, CAPTAIN
TRAINING SUPERVISOR

Heihachiro Nogura

HEIHACHIRO NOGURA
COMMANDER STARFLEET

WHundert

WILLIAM HUNDERT
COMMANDANT STARFLEET ACADEMY

SPOCK FU
A LOGICAL ALTERNATIVE TO KIRK FU

VULCAN NERVE PINCH

Step 1: Approach opponent from behind. Utilize stealth to ensure target is not alerted to your presence.

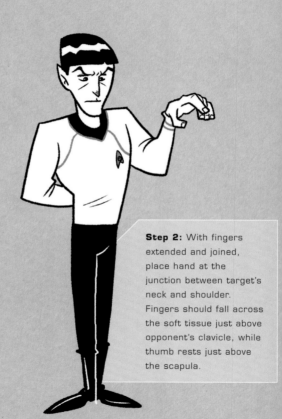

Step 2: With fingers extended and joined, place hand at the junction between target's neck and shoulder. Fingers should fall across the soft tissue just above opponent's clavicle, while thumb rests just above the scapula.

This assumes your opponent possesses a superior transverse ligament. Beings who lack this or a similar physiological feature, or who have undergone specific genetic engineering or other training, may prove resistant to this technique. Results may vary.

Step 3: Apply steady, firm pressure along target's superior transverse ligament. Be prepared to support adversary's weight when their body goes limp after they react to the nervous system overload.

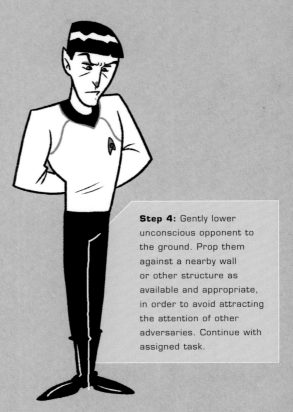

Step 4: Gently lower unconscious opponent to the ground. Prop them against a nearby wall or other structure as available and appropriate, in order to avoid attracting the attention of other adversaries. Continue with assigned task.

TITAN
BOOKS

144 Southwark Street
London SE1 0UP
www.titanbooks.com

Find us on Facebook: www.facebook.com/titanbooks

Follow us on Twitter: @TitanBooks

™ & © 2020 CBS Studios Inc. STAR TREK and related marks and logos are trademarks of CBS Studios Inc. All Rights Reserved.

Published by Titan Books, London, in 2020.

No part of this book may be reproduced in any form without written permission from the publisher.

Library of Congress Cataloging-in-Publication Data available.

ISBN: 978-1-78909-497-8

Publisher: Raoul Goff
President: Kate Jerome
Associate Publisher: Vanessa Lopez
Creative Director: Chrissy Kwasnik
Designer: Evelyn Furuta
Senior Editor: Kelly Reed
Managing Editor: Lauren LePera
Senior Production Editor: Rachel Anderson
Senior Production Manager: Greg Steffen

Illustrations by Christian Cornia

ROOTS of PEACE   REPLANTED PAPER

Insight Editions, in association with Roots of Peace, will plant two trees for each tree used in the manufacturing of this book. Roots of Peace is an internationally renowned humanitarian organization dedicated to eradicating land mines worldwide and converting war-torn lands into productive farms and wildlife habitats. Roots of Peace will plant two million fruit and nut trees in Afghanistan and provide farmers there with the skills and support necessary for sustainable land use.

Manufactured in China by Insight Editions

10 9 8 7 6 5 4 3 2 1

ABOUT THE AUTHOR

Dayton Ward is the *New York Times* best-selling author or coauthor of numerous novels and short stories, including a whole bunch of stuff set in the Star Trek universe, and often works with friend and cowriter Kevin Dilmore. He lives in Kansas City with his wife and two daughters. Find Dayton on the web at www.daytonward.com.

ABOUT THE ILLUSTRATOR

Christian Cornia is an Italian artist who has created designs for many publishers, advertisers, video games, and role-playing games. He currently works with the international illustration agency Advocate Art and teaches character animation design at the Reggio Emilia International School of Comics. Christian's most notable work includes several *Scooby-Doo* projects, inking for Marvel Comics, and illustrating the graphic novel *Brina*, which was published by Tunué in 2017. More artwork at www.christiancornia.it